AR Quiz
IL _MG_

BL _6.1_

Pts. _1_

Let Freedom Ring

The War of 1812

by Susan E. Haberle

Consultant:
Dr. Larry L. Nelson, Site Manager
Fort Meigs State Memorial
Ohio Historical Society
Perrysburg, Ohio

Bridgestone Books
an imprint of Capstone Press
Mankato, Minnesota

Bridgestone Books are published by Capstone Press
151 Good Counsel Drive, P.O. Box 669, Mankato, Minnesota 56002
http://www.capstone-press.com

Library of Congress Cataloging-in-Publication Data
Haberle, Susan E.
   The War of 1812 / by Susan E. Haberle.
      v. cm. — (Let freedom ring)
   Includes bibliographical references and index.
   Contents: Causes of the war—Early battles—Victories on the
water—Washington, D.C., and Baltimore—Final battles
   Summary: Traces the causes and effects of the War of 1812,
including its effect on relations between the United States and
Great Britain.
   ISBN 0-7368-1560-0 (hardcover)
   1. United States—History—War of 1812—Juvenile literature.
[1. United States—History—War of 1812.] I. Title. II. Series.

E354 .H33 2003
973.5'2—dc21   2002012005

Editorial Credits
Charles Pederson, editor; Kia Adams, series designer; Juliette Peters,
book designer; Kelly Garvin, photo researcher; Karen Risch, product
planning editor

Photo Credits
Corbis/Bettmann, 30
ImageState, Inc./Brent Winebrenner, 25
North Wind Picture Archives, cover (small), 5, 7, 11, 15, 19, 20, 22, 27, 29,
    39, 40, 42, 43
Ohio Historical Society, 8
Stock Montage, Inc., cover (main), 13, 17, 35, 37

1   2   3   4   5   6   08   07   06   05   04   03

Table of Contents

Chapter One

The War Begins

Some people call the War of 1812 (1812–1814) the second Revolutionary War. The British did not like losing their American colonies after the first Revolutionary War (1775–1783). After that war, the United States and Great Britain were not friendly. By 1812, the United States and Great Britain were ready for another war with each other.

In 1812, U.S. President James Madison supported going to war with Great Britain for three reasons. First, the British were taking sailors from U.S. ships and forcing them to serve in the British navy. This practice was called impressment. Second, Great Britain had set up trade barriers against the United States. Third, the British supported American Indian attacks against western U.S. settlers.

Impressment

Between 1793 and 1812, the British impressed more than 15,000 U.S. sailors to serve on British ships. When boarding American ships, the British

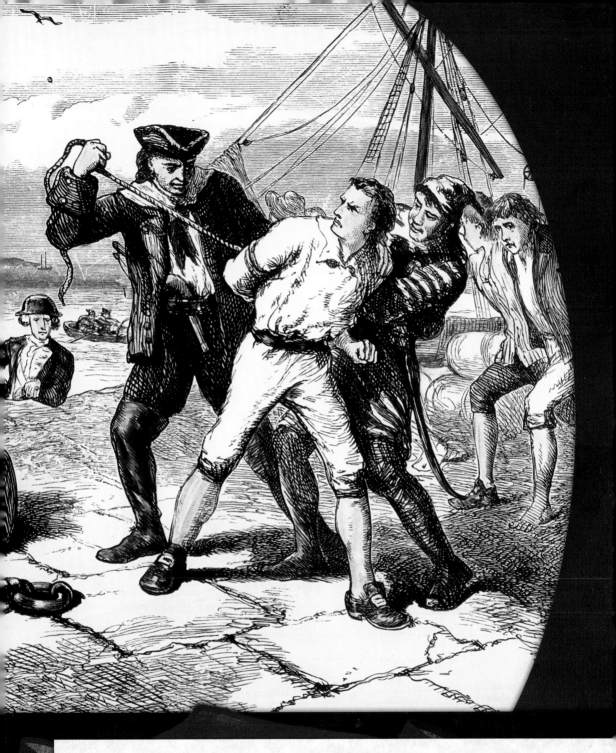

In the early 1800s, British sailors forced U.S. citizens to serve in the British navy. This impressment was one cause of the War of 1812.

claimed they were looking for British sailors who had left the British navy. Often, they captured U.S. sailors. These sailors said the British officers often punished them. When British ships approached, some U.S. sailors jumped from their ships into the water to escape impressment.

In June 1807, sailors from the British warship *Leopard* tried to board the U.S. ship *Chesapeake* to look for deserters. The U.S.S. *Chesapeake*'s officers would not let the British board, so the British began firing their cannons at the *Chesapeake*. Angered by this action, U.S. citizens began to support a war against Great Britain.

Trade Barriers

The United States also was caught between two countries. Since 1793, Great Britain and France had been at war. Both countries wanted the United States to stop trading with the other country.

Trade was important to the United States. U.S. merchants sold wheat, corn, cotton, and wood products to European countries. In return, they bought European clothing, tools, sugar, coffee, and spices. By the early 1800s, the United States had more trading ships at sea than any other country except Great Britain. When the United States ignored the wishes of France and Great Britain, the British navy began to stop U.S. trading ships from sailing.

After the British attack on the *Chesapeake,* the U.S. Congress passed the Embargo Act in December 1807. This law was supposed to punish Great Britain. It actually stopped the United States from selling goods to or buying goods from other countries. U.S. businesses could not sell their products abroad, so the British could not buy U.S. goods from any nation.

American docks stood empty. Merchants could not sell their goods after the United States passed the Embargo Act of 1807.

The Embargo Act was a failure. The law did not hurt Great Britain, but it did hurt American merchants. Many shipbuilders and sailors lost their jobs because no ships were needed for trade. Lumber companies that supplied wood for shipbuilding closed. Farmers who depended on international trade could not sell their food. In 1809, Congress took back the Embargo Act. The United States once again could trade with other nations.

By signing the Treaty of Greenville, Indians agreed to give up land in exchange for money from the U.S. government. White settlers moved onto these Indian lands.

Trade with American Indians

American Indians trapped and killed animals for their fur, which they traded to Europeans. In return for furs, the Indians received blankets, clothing, weapons, gunpowder, tools, tobacco, dyes, and jewelry. The Indians traded mostly beaver furs, which were popular for making hats.

American Indians

The 1795 Treaty of Greenville gave American Indians money in exchange for land in what is now Ohio and Indiana. The treaty opened the Northwest Territory for white settlement. This territory included present-day Ohio, Indiana, Illinois, Michigan, Wisconsin, and eastern Minnesota. The treaty ended 20 years of fighting between the settlers and the Indians in that area.

U.S. settlers still took land from the Indians beyond what was allowed by the treaty. In this area, farming and beaver hunting were good. Many Indian nations turned to the British for help against the settlers. During the Revolutionary War, the British had helped some Indian nations by providing money and weapons. By helping the Indians, the British hoped the Indians would keep U.S. settlers and traders out of the northwest.

A Nation Divided

People in the United States disagreed about going to war. Some members of Congress wanted war. These men were known as War Hawks. They wanted to expand U.S. borders and take over British Canada. They also wanted Florida, which Spain claimed.

The United States was poorly prepared for war. The U.S. Navy had few ships, and the army numbered only 7,000 poorly trained soldiers. The state militias did not have enough volunteers trained to fight. Members of the militia were less trained than soldiers. Militiamen also served a shorter time than regular soldiers. Many army leaders were former Revolutionary War leaders who lacked the energy of young leaders. War money was scarce.

On June 18, 1812, President Madison and the U.S. Congress declared war against Great Britain. Madison did not know the British had already decided to stop interfering with U.S. shipping. Because the news traveled slowly from Europe,

U.S. leaders did not know for several weeks about Great Britain's decision. By then, war had begun, which made the British angry.

Many people in New England did not support the war. They called it "Mr. Madison's war," because President Madison supported it. Some people in New England flew their flags at half-staff when war was declared. Flying their flags in this way showed they were unhappy about the war. Many people in the area refused to volunteer to serve in the military. Some New England people supplied cattle to the British in Canada so the British would have more food.

Blue-coated U.S. soldiers served in the War of 1812. At the war's start, the army numbered only about 7,000 men.

Chapter Two

Early Battles

The first major fight of the War of 1812 took place before the war officially began. This was the Battle of Tippecanoe. The battle had a major effect on American Indians who fought on the side of Great Britain.

The Shawnee Indian leader, Tecumseh, wanted to unite all Indian nations east of the Mississippi River. His goal was to regain Indian land taken by U.S. settlers. He asked his brother, Tenskwatawa, to help.

Tenskwatawa was called "The Prophet." He got this name because he claimed the Master of All Life sent him visions. One vision concerned protecting the Shawnee way of life. Together, Tecumseh and Tenskwatawa started a town called Prophetstown on the Tippecanoe River in northern Indiana.

U.S. leaders worried about Tecumseh's growing power. William Henry Harrison, governor of the Indiana Territory, worried the Indians might join the British

The soldiers of William Henry Harrison fought the forces of Tecumseh and Tenskwatawa at the Battle of Tippecanoe.

in Canada. He feared they might drive U.S. settlers from the Ohio River Valley. Harrison ordered Fort Harrison built to protect settlers in the territory.

On November 7, 1811, Harrison led 1,000 men to Prophetstown. Tecumseh was away trying to convince more warriors to join his group. Tenskwatawa convinced his followers to fight Harrison's army. At the Battle of Tippecanoe, Harrison's army destroyed the town and forced the Indians living there to leave. Many of them joined their British allies in Canada.

Controlling the Waterways

Many early battles of the War of 1812 took place along waterways. The Great Lakes and other major waterways were important to the United States for travel and trade. Some of Great Britain's forts around the Great Lakes were actually located inside the United States. British troops at the forts were able to stop Americans from trading and traveling.

The first official battle of the war was at Fort Detroit, in present-day Michigan. In July 1812, U.S. General William Hull led 2,000 soldiers to Fort Detroit. From there, he planned to attack nearby

Fort Malden, located in Ontario, Canada. He hoped the attack on Fort Malden would force British troops to leave Lake Huron and Lake Erie. Hull hoped the Indians would leave with the British.

Instead of leaving, British commander Isaac Brock learned of Hull's plan and ordered an attack on Fort Detroit. On August 16, British soldiers and Tecumseh's warriors attacked. The fort was well defended, but Hull had brought his family there. He decided to surrender the fort without firing a

General William Hull was a leader in the U.S. Army. In 1812, he planned to lead an attack on Fort Malden, Ontario.

shot because he was worried about his family's safety. After the Battle of Fort Detroit, the British controlled Lake Huron and Lake Erie.

The Battle of Fort Detroit gave the Indians hope for regaining their land. They saw the weakness of the U.S. Army. Many more Indians joined the British forces.

In October 1812, another battle took place. U.S. soldiers at Fort Niagara, New York, were forced to surrender to British forces.

After the Battle of Fort Niagara, U.S. soldiers planned to attack the British at Lake Champlain in New York. U.S. Army leaders decided not even to begin that battle. They believed the U.S. soldiers were too weak to fight the British.

Women in the War

Some women disguised themselves as men so they could serve in the war. One British widow, Almira Paul, wanted revenge for the death of her husband, a British soldier. Paul disguised herself in her husband's clothes and became a cook's helper on a British ship. For three years, no one knew she was a woman. Twice, U.S. forces captured her and beat her. She wrote in her journal, "I'm pleased to think to what length a female might carry her adventures, what hardships she could endure and what dangers brave, and all without betraying her sex!"

Other women like the one below fought alongside men without disguising themselves. Women made bags to hold gunpowder, helped pack ammunition, and carried cannonballs to men firing the cannons.

Chapter Three

Victories on the Water

The U.S. Navy had only 20 warships, while Great Britain had 600. Battle far out at sea was impossible because the British ships would have quickly defeated the U.S. ships. Instead, U.S. ships stayed in harbors or near the Atlantic shore to fight the British. The fighting was often so close to land that people on shore could watch.

In spite of being small, the U.S. Navy enjoyed some important victories. In the first six months of the war, the United States captured 450 British ships. Many U.S. Navy ships were smaller and faster than most British ships. The navy destroyed some British ships in battle and captured others to add to its fleet. The U.S. Navy defeated the British near Canada and in the Caribbean Sea south of Spanish Florida. These victories improved the spirits of U.S. troops and increased the number of ships in the navy.

After victories at sea, U.S. sailors boarded enemy ships.

In August 1812, the U.S. Navy claimed a victory. The U.S.S. *Constitution* fought a battle against the British ship *Guerriere* in the North Atlantic Ocean. Captain Isaac Hull took command of the *Constitution* in New York Harbor. Hull was a fearless fighter who had fought pirates in the Caribbean Sea and near North Africa.

During the battle, the *Guerriere* fired its cannons at the *Constitution*, but the cannonballs bounced off the *Constitution*'s hard oak side. As a result, sailors began to call the *Constitution* "Old Ironsides." The soldiers on the ship went on to win

The U.S.S. *Constitution*, left, battled the British ship *Guerriere* in the Atlantic Ocean. During the battle, British cannonballs bounced off the *Constitution*'s side. Afterward, sailors called the ship "Old Ironsides."

the first big victory for the United States. It proved that U.S. sailors could fight effectively.

The British also had some naval victories. In June 1813, the British ship *Shannon* fought the U.S.S. *Chesapeake*. This was the same ship that had resisted a British attack in 1807. The two ships sailed toward each other. When their cannons were in range, both ships simply blasted them at each other. The *Shannon* won the battle. During the fighting, *Chesapeake* captain James Lawrence was wounded. Before he died, his last words to his men were, "Don't give up the ship."

The Battle of Lake Erie

In 1813, the U.S. government sent naval commander Oliver Perry to Lake Erie to break the British blockade of the lake. British ships were sailing Lake Erie to prevent U.S. ships from using it to protect settlers and supply troops. Perry's orders were to defeat the British fleet and take control of the lake.

On September 10, 1813, the British and American ships approached each other. In the late morning, the Battle of Lake Erie began. The big British guns began to fire on the ships in Perry's fleet. For several hours, the British cannons battered Perry's command ship, the U.S.S. *Lawrence,* until it could no longer fight. Instead of surrendering, Perry boarded a small rowboat and crossed to another ship in his fleet. From there, he ordered a renewed attack on the British ships. In 15 minutes, his ships had destroyed the British fleet.

The Battle of Lake Erie changed the course of the war. Afterward, the U.S. Navy controlled the lake. British General Henry Procter ordered his troops to leave Fort Malden and march into Canada

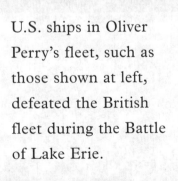

U.S. ships in Oliver Perry's fleet, such as those shown at left, defeated the British fleet during the Battle of Lake Erie.

because they could no longer receive supplies by ship. Perry's victory at Lake Erie raised confidence, protected the Northwest Territory, and opened supply lines for U.S. citizens.

The Battle of the Thames River

After Procter retreated, the Shawnee leader, Tecumseh, became angry. He wanted the British to defeat the United States. After that, he hoped the British would return land his people had earlier lost during the Battle of Tippecanoe. Instead, Tecumseh was forced to leave with the British. The Indians and British moved north up the Thames River, intending to join British troops at Fort Niagara.

On October 5, 1813, about 400 British soldiers and 1,200 Indians were stationed near Fort Malden at Moraviantown, Ontario. Harrison and 3,500 U.S. troops attacked. During the Battle of the Thames River, most of the British soldiers surrendered. Tecumseh's warriors continued to fight in hand-to-hand combat. An unknown U.S. soldier shot and killed Tecumseh. Tecumseh's death discouraged his followers, who retreated. Harrison's army won the battle.

A British Blockade

Great Britain blockaded the East Coast to prevent U.S. ships from getting in and out of the harbors. The British goal was to keep ships from trading or from leaving harbors to attack the British navy. At first, the blockade did not include New England because the New England states had opposed the war. They depended on trade with Great Britain and feared war would hurt their merchants and farmers.

The British hoped the people of New England would join them in the war. New Englanders refused to join, so Great Britain also blockaded towns and harbors along the New England coast. Merchants and farmers could not ship products or receive imported goods. This condition encouraged New Englanders to support the U.S. war effort.

The U.S.S. *Constitution*

Between 1794 and 1797, Boston shipbuilders built the U.S.S. *Constitution*. George Washington named the ship after the Constitution of the United States. The ship was made from more than 1,500 trees grown from Maine to Georgia. The ship carried cannons made in Rhode Island and copper fastenings that Revolutionary War hero Paul Revere provided.

Called "Old Ironsides," the ship sailed on missions for more than 100 years and was never defeated in battle. In 1934, it came home to Boston Harbor. Today, the *Constitution*, below, is in the U.S.S. *Constitution* Museum. It is part of the Boston National Historical Park at the Charlestown Navy Yard.

Chapter Four

Washington, D.C., and Baltimore

During the War of 1812, Great Britain fought France in Europe. In April 1814, France lost a major battle and ended the European war. After the war with France ended, Great Britain could turn its military attention to North America. It sent 14,000 more troops to fight against the United States.

In August 1814, several thousand British troops sailed into the Chesapeake Bay and up the Potomac River between Virginia and Maryland. Their goal was to attack Washington, D.C. The attack surprised many U.S. leaders. They thought the target would be Baltimore, Maryland, because that was an important harbor city with many ships. Leaders were not prepared for the attack on inland Washington, D.C.

On the evening of August 24, 1814, the British met little military resistance when they arrived in Washington, D.C.

Before the War of 1812, Washington, D.C., was a peaceful, small town. The 1814 British attack on the town surprised U.S. military leaders.

The British soldiers used axes to destroy buildings belonging to the government. They then set fire to the buildings, burning down the Senate, the Treasury, and the House of Representatives. They also set fire to the navy yard and all of the ships docked there at the time. The flames were so bright, people could see them 137 miles (220 kilometers) away in Philadelphia, Pennsylvania.

Burning the White House

At the White House, Dolley Madison, the wife of the president, had prepared a big dinner. Hearing about the attack, she had to escape quickly, leaving behind the dinner. When British troops arrived to burn the White House, their officers first sat and ate the dinner themselves.

As Madison left, she saved some historical items from the White House. She took a famous life-size portrait of George Washington. She had a worker break the painting's heavy frame to get it out in time. She also took copies of important government papers. Madison said if she did not take these items, "the British would be pleased to burn" them.

The attack on Washington, D.C., lowered the spirits of U.S. citizens, but it also united the people against their British enemy. More people began to support the war.

The Attack on Baltimore

In September 1814, British Vice Admiral Alexander Cochrane led 50 British ships carrying 4,500 troops up the Chesapeake Bay to the Patapsco River in Maryland. The troops planned to attack the important harbor city of Baltimore.

During the attack on Washington, D.C., the British army burned many government buildings.

Unlike the people of Washington, D.C., the people of Baltimore were prepared. About 16,000 U.S. troops and hundreds of armed citizens waited for the British.

The military commander in Baltimore, General Samuel Smith, wanted to protect the city. He purposely sank empty boats near Fort McHenry. This fort guarded the entrance to Baltimore Harbor. The sunken boats blocked the large British ships from entering the harbor. The British could not sail close enough to Baltimore to use their cannons. To clear the sunken ships and attack the city, the British first had to capture Fort McHenry.

The British navy bombed Fort McHenry during its attack on Baltimore.

The Fort McHenry Flag

In 1813, U.S. leaders asked Mary Young Pickersgill to sew a military flag. In 1814, her flag flew over Fort McHenry and inspired Francis Scott Key to write "The Star-Spangled Banner." Pickersgill was a Baltimore widow who lived with her daughter, Caroline. The flag Pickersgill sewed was 30 feet (9.1 meters) wide and 42 feet (13 meters) long. Each of its 15 stars was 2 feet (.6 meter) wide.

Pickersgill started sewing the flag at home but soon realized her house was too small. She assembled the flag on the floor of a nearby brewery during the evenings when the workers were gone. Pickersgill and Caroline worked several weeks and finished the flag by candlelight. The government paid Pickersgill $405.90 for her work.

In the years after the Battle of Fort McHenry, soldiers' widows asked for pieces of the flag to bury with their husbands. Today, the remains of the Fort McHenry flag are displayed in the Smithsonian Institution's National Museum of American History in Washington, D.C.

When the attack began on Fort McHenry, Francis Scott Key, a Washington, D.C., lawyer, was arranging an exchange of prisoners. He was aboard a British ship near the fort. Key worried about the U.S. soldiers in the fort.

Key believed the battle for Baltimore was not lost as long as the U.S. flag flew over Fort McHenry. If the flag still flew, that meant the soldiers had not surrendered. Through a telescope, Key watched during the night as British ships fired 2,000 cannonballs at Fort McHenry. He could see the flag only when the glare from these bombs lit the sky. The next morning, Key saw the flag was still flying. He knew the British military had not defeated the U.S. soldiers.

The sight of the flag moved Key to write a poem called "Defence of Fort M'Henry." Two years later, he set the poem to music and changed its name to "The Star-Spangled Banner." In 1931, the song became the U.S. national anthem.

On September 24, 1814, the British decided they could not capture the fort and stopped the attack on Baltimore. The battle was a major victory for the United States.

The War of 1812

MINNESOTA

Lake Superior

Lake Huron

CANADA
(Great Britain)

Lake Champlain

Lake Champlain

WISCONSIN

Lake Michigan

Fort Niagara

Lake Ontario

NEW YORK

MICHIGAN

Thames River
Fort Malden

Lake Erie

New York City

Fort Detroit

Lake Erie

Prophetstown

Tippecanoe River

OHIO

Baltimore

Fort McHenry

Washington, D.C.

MARYLAND

Mississippi River

ILLINOIS

INDIANA

Ohio River

VIRGINIA

Chesapeake Bay

UNITED STATES

ATLANTIC OCEAN

ALABAMA

Horseshoe Bend

Tallapoosa River

LOUISIANA

Fort Mims

MEXICO
(Spain)

New Orleans

FLORIDA
(Spain)

N
W E
S

LEGEND

United States

Land Claimed by Spain

Land Claimed by Great Britain

Northwest Territory

Other U.S. Territory

Battle Site

Chapter Five

Final Battles

Like many American Indians, Creek warriors fought alongside British soldiers during the War of 1812. Among the most powerful Indian nations, the Creek occupied lands in present-day Alabama and Mississippi. Some people called Creek warriors "Red Sticks" because of their red war clubs.

On August 29, 1813, Creek Chief Red Eagle led an attack at Fort Mims, north of Mobile, Alabama. They wanted to regain land they had lost. The attack surprised U.S. troops. Most of the 600 white soldiers and civilians at the fort were killed.

When the U.S. government heard of the attack, it sent 3,500 militiamen, 1,000 foot soldiers, and many Tennessee mounted soldiers. Andrew Jackson led these troops, which included famous congressman and explorer Davy Crockett. During what came to be known as the Red Stick War, U.S. forces fought the Creek at several battles in Alabama.

Creek Red Stick warriors attacked U.S. soldiers and civilians during the Battle of Fort Mims.

In March 1814, the Battle of Horseshoe Bend was fought. This final battle of the Red Stick War took place along the Tallapoosa River in Alabama. About 900 Red Stick warriors faced 2,000 U.S. soldiers. The U.S. forces trapped the Creek near a sharp bend in the river. The Americans killed or wounded about 500 Creek during the battle. As a result of their defeat, the Creek had to give up about 23 million acres (9.3 million hectares) of land.

The war with the Creek was important to the United States for two reasons. First, it ended most Indian resistance during the War of 1812. Second, it prevented the Creek from helping the British during the later Battle of New Orleans.

In September 1814, the British invaded New York from the north across Lake Champlain. The stronger U.S. Army defeated them. By then, Great Britain wanted to end the war.

On December 24, 1814, the United States and Great Britain signed the Treaty of Ghent days before the Battle of New Orleans. News traveled slowly across the Atlantic Ocean, and battles continued for a few weeks even after the peace treaty was signed.

Red Eagle's Surrender

According to legend, Red Eagle, below right, walked alone into the U.S. camp after the 1814 Battle of Horseshoe Bend. Born as Bill Weatherford, Red Eagle said to the seated Andrew Jackson: "I am Bill Weatherford. I am in your power, do with me as you please. I am a soldier. I have done the white people all the harm I could; I have fought them, and fought them bravely; if I had an army, I would yet fight, . . . but I have none; my people are all gone. I can do no more than weep over the misfortunes of my nation."

Jackson was impressed. He released Red Eagle, who kept his word and never again fought the United States.

The Battle of New Orleans

British troops wanted to control the mouth of the Mississippi River, located at New Orleans, in present-day Louisiana. The river was important for trade and transportation. The British believed they could block U.S. expansion. Winning a battle at New Orleans would give the British control of the river.

In late December 1814, the British took over a large farm south of New Orleans. There, they planned their attack on the city. In January 1815, they attacked New Orleans with 5,000 men and 50 ships.

Andrew Jackson was in charge of defending the city. With him were more than 4,000 troops, including African Americans, French, Jews, and Germans. The army even included a few pirates under the command of a man named Jean Lafitte. This mixed army reflected the city's diverse population. Jackson brought in 2,500 fighters from Tennessee and Kentucky. So many different groups were part of the army that people called it a ragtag band of soldiers.

The Battle of New Orleans was fought for three weeks in swamps, creeks, and marshy, winding rivers. The countryside made it difficult for the enemy soldiers to see each other. Even though the British soldiers outnumbered the U.S. troops, they were no match for the U.S. fighters. The final battle lasted only one hour. The United States lost 13 men, while the British lost 500.

The blue-coated American defenders defeated the red-coated British army during the Battle of New Orleans.

The War Nobody Won

The War of 1812 has been called "the war nobody won." All British and American boundaries between the two countries were returned to where they had been before 1812. There was no change in free trade or the rights of sailors. More than 2,000 U.S. citizens died in battle and another 4,000 were wounded. Thousands of British soldiers were killed or wounded.

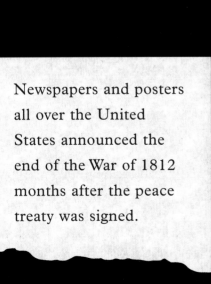

Newspapers and posters all over the United States announced the end of the War of 1812 months after the peace treaty was signed.

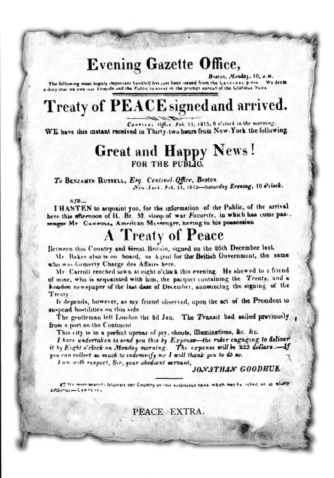

A Better International Reputation

"The war raised our reputation in Europe, and [the Europeans are surprised] that we . . . fought Great Britain single handed . . . I think it will be a long time before we are disturbed again by any of the powers of Europe."

—James Bayard, U.S. political leader, in a letter to his son

Yet, the war was important for the United States. The war gave U.S. citizens a new sense of national pride and unity. The U.S. Army and U.S. Navy became more experienced. After the war, other countries had more respect for the United States and began to view it as a world power.

Of all the groups fighting in the war, American Indians lost the most. They lost important leaders and much of their land east of the Mississippi River. Their British support was gone. Many Indian nations were forced to move west of the Mississippi River.

TIMELINE

The British impress American sailors into the British navy.

June: The *Chesapeake* and *Leopard* battle.

| 1793–1812 | 1807 | 1811 |

The United States passes the Embargo Act.

The Battle of Tippecanoe is fought.

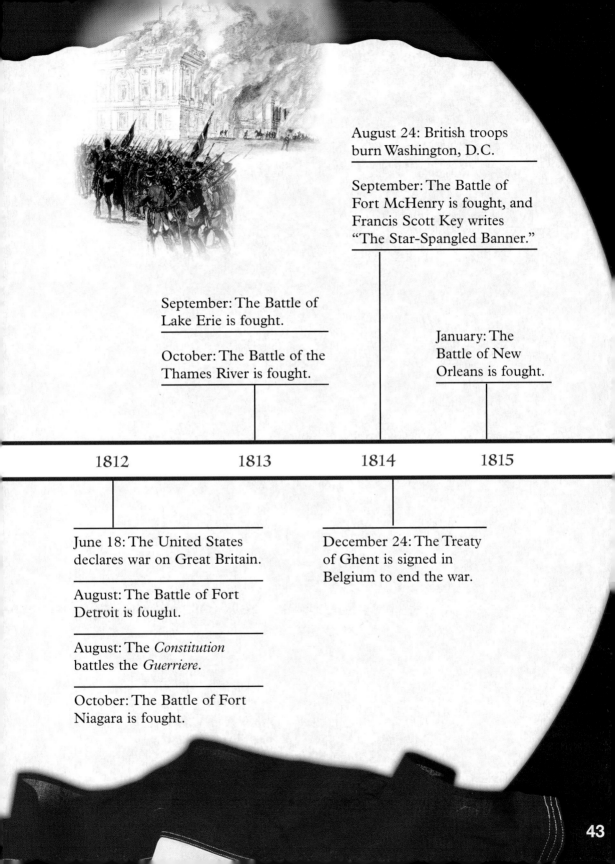

August 24: British troops burn Washington, D.C.

September: The Battle of Fort McHenry is fought, and Francis Scott Key writes "The Star-Spangled Banner."

September: The Battle of Lake Erie is fought.

October: The Battle of the Thames River is fought.

January: The Battle of New Orleans is fought.

| 1812 | 1813 | 1814 | 1815 |

June 18: The United States declares war on Great Britain.

August: The Battle of Fort Detroit is fought.

August: The *Constitution* battles the *Guerriere*.

October: The Battle of Fort Niagara is fought.

December 24: The Treaty of Ghent is signed in Belgium to end the war.

Glossary

blockade (blok-ADE)—the prevention of ships from getting into or out of a harbor

impressment (im-PRESS-muhnt)—the act of forcing someone to serve in the military

independence (in-di-PEN-duhnss)—freedom; the state of self-government

militia (muh-LISH-uh)—a group of citizens trained to fight in military emergencies

Northwest Territory (north-WEST TER-uh-tor-ee)—land purchased from the American Indians that now includes Ohio, Indiana, Illinois, Michigan, Wisconsin, and eastern Minnesota

treaty (TREE-tee)—a formal agreement between two or more groups or governments

War Hawks (WOR HAWKSS)—U.S. congressmen in favor of going to war in 1812

For Further Reading

Gregson, Susan R. *Tecumseh: Shawnee Leader.* Let Freedom Ring. Mankato, Minn.: Bridgestone Books, 2003.

Kelley, Brent P. *James Madison: Father of the Constitution.* Revolutionary War Leaders. Philadelphia: Chelsea House, 2001.

King, David C. *New Orleans.* Battlefields across America. Brookfield, Conn.: Twenty-First Century Books, 1998.

Santella, Andrew. *The War of 1812.* Cornerstones of Freedom. New York: Children's Press, 2001.

Stefoff, Rebecca. *The War of 1812.* North American Historical Atlases. New York: Benchmark Books. 2001.

Thro, Ellen, and Andrew K. Frank. *Growing and Dividing: The Making of America.* Austin, Texas: Raintree Steck-Vaughn, 2001.

Todd, Anne M. *The War of 1812.* America Goes to War. Mankato, Minn.: Capstone Books, 2000.

Places of Interest

Fort Malden National Historic Site of Canada
100 Laird Avenue
P.O. Box 38
Amherstburg, ON N9V 2Z2
Canada

The Battle of the Thames River was fought near this historic site.

Fort McHenry National Monument and Historic Shrine
End of East Fort Avenue
Baltimore, MD 21230-5393

At this monument, visitors may take self-guided tours or see a living history demonstration of life during the War of 1812.

Horseshoe Bend National Military Park
11288 Horseshoe Bend Road
Daviston, AL 36256-9751

Visitors can camp in the park or visit the museum.

Old Fort Niagara Association
P.O. Box 169
Youngstown, NY 14174-0169

This group has preserved some of the original forts used during the War of 1812.

Tippecanoe Battlefield
State Road 43
North of Lafayette, Indiana
For information, write to
The Tippecanoe County
Historical Association
909 South Street
Lafayette, IN 47901

The Battle of Tippecanoe was fought at this site. A visitors' center houses a museum.

U.S.S. *Constitution* Museum
P.O. Box 1812
Boston, MA 02129

Visitors can see "Old Ironsides" and learn about its battles.

Internet Sites

Do you want to learn more about the War of 1812?
Visit the FACT HOUND at *http://www.facthound.com*

FACT HOUND can track down many sites to help you.
All the FACT HOUND sites are hand-selected
by Capstone Press editors. FACT HOUND will fetch the best,
most accurate information to answer your questions.

IT IS EASY! IT IS FUN!
1) Go to *http://www.facthound.com*
2) Type in: 0736815600
3) Click on "FETCH IT," and
   FACT HOUND will put you
   on the trail of several helpful links.

You can also search by subject or book title. So, relax
and let our pal FACT HOUND do the research for you!

Index